W9-BOF-917

LEONTYNE PRICE
Opera Superstar

By Sylvia B. Williams

CHILDRENS PRESS ™

CHICAGO

To my mother, Arbelle W. Barkemeyer

Picture Acknowledgments

Cover: Leontyne Price as Lenora in Verdi's *Il Trovatore*
©J. Heffernan

Courtesy Ms. Leontyne Price—6, 15, 21, 25 (top)

Bettmann Archive, Inc.—17

©Jack Mitchell—2, 25 (bottom)

Courtesy Oak Park High School, Laurel, Mississippi

©Hugh Dilworth and Metropolitan Opera Association

Brown Brothers—26

The New York Public Library—28

UPI—10

Wide World—12 (two photos), 20 (two photos), 27, 30

Library of Congress Cataloging in Publication Data

Williams, Sylvia B.
    Leontyne Price, opera superstar.

    (Picture-story biographies)
    Summary: A brief biography of the black opera singer
who is one of the most celebrated sopranos of her time
and who, among other honors, opened the inaugural
season of the new Metropolitan Opera House.
    1. Price, Leontyne—Juvenile literature. 2. Singers—
United States—Biography—Juvenile literature.
[1. Price, Leontyne. 2. Singers. 3. Afro-Americans—
Biography] I. Title. II. Series.
ML420.P97W54 1984   782.1'092'4   [B]   84-7617
ISBN 0-516-03531-2

LEONTYNE PRICE
Opera Superstar

Sincerely,
Leontyne Price

"Leontyne!" No answer.

"Leontyne, time to practice your piano lessons."

"Coming, Mother!"

Six-year-old Leontyne Price did not mind leaving her friends and their game of hopscotch. She did not mind coming inside to practice her music lessons. In fact, she loved practicing the piano.

When Leontyne was a young child in Laurel, Mississippi, it was clear that she had musical talent. Mrs. Price, her mother, was a talented singer in the church choir. She wanted to do everything she could to develop her daughter's talent. She involved Leontyne in music at home, at school, and at church. Music soon was Leontyne's life.

Leontyne began taking piano lessons when she was five years old. She was six when she was presented in her first recital by her piano teacher, Mrs. Hattie McInnis.

Until this time Mr. Price, Leontyne's father, had had little interest in her music lessons. But after hearing Leontyne perform, he changed his mind. Smiling from ear to ear, he said, "I'm so proud of my little girl!" From then on he helped Leontyne in every way he could.

An exciting surprise awaited Leontyne on her sixth birthday. Her parents had saved enough to buy a secondhand piano. Finally Leontyne had a piano of her very own!

Leontyne had a brother named George who was two years younger. Mrs. Price wanted George to learn to play the piano, too. George started taking lessons from Mrs. McInnis. Although he learned to play several songs with his sister, George did not enjoy playing at all. He told his mother he would rather play football. Piano lessons for him were stopped.

Retired Brigadier General George C. Price holds the Distinguished Patriot Award given to him by the Women's National Republic Club in 1983. Leontyne Price sang at the award ceremony.

George later became a football star in high school and college. He joined the armed services after college and became a brigadier general in the United States Army.

Leontyne went to Sandy Gavin Elementary School, where she also learned dancing and acrobatics from her third-grade teacher. She loved performing and was often the star in many of the school programs. She always took great care with her schoolwork, too, and was an A student.

Marian Anderson sang on the Voice of America radio program in 1953.
In 1955, she became the first black soloist to sing with the Metropolitan Opera
Company. After a triumphant farewell concert at Carnegie Hall,
she retired from the stage in 1965.

When Leontyne was nine years old, her mother took her by bus to Jackson, Mississippi, to hear Marian Anderson in concert. Marian Anderson was the first black singer to appear at New York City's Metropolitan Opera. Leontyne was thrilled and inspired. She decided that she wanted to be an artist like Marian Anderson.

Leontyne sent this autographed photograph to Oak Park High School thanking the school for giving her a "wonderful beginning."

Leontyne next entered Oak Park Vocational High School, an all-black institution rated as one of the best high schools in Mississippi. She quickly became a leader at school.

Leontyne sang first soprano with the Oak Park choral group. She also played for many school concerts and church and community programs. Before she graduated from high school, Leontyne appeared in a solo recital, singing as well as playing the piano.

Leontyne was very active in school activities and well liked by her teachers and classmates. She graduated with honors and was presented with an award for outstanding ability in music.

Mr. and Mrs. Price were convinced that Leontyne should continue her education. They arranged for her to attend Wilberforce College (now Central State University) in Ohio. Wilberforce was the first black university to be established in the United States.

Leontyne was on a scholarship and worked part-time to help with the expenses.

Leontyne as she appeared as Elvira in the opera *Ernani* at the Metropolitan Opera.

It was a memorable day when Leontyne boarded the train to leave home for the first time to attend college. It was hard leaving her family, friends, and home. But Leontyne knew that she could not stay in Laurel and still hope to follow the plans she had made for her future.

When Leontyne began college she had no idea of the full potential of her vocal ability. Her goal at that time was to get a degree and teach music. Then she could help out at home and help pay her brother's way through college.

Leontyne did not forget her religious training after she left home. She continued to attend church services regularly and sing in the choir. Often she would have happy memories of services at Saint Paul Methodist Church in Laurel. Influenced by her devout Christian mother and father, she always says a little prayer before going on stage.

Catherine Van Buren was Leontyne's first voice coach. Impressed by her enthusiasm and ability to learn quickly, Ms. Van Buren encouraged Leontyne to

Leontyne must spend
long hours of practice
with and without
the orchestra before
any performance.

obtain the advanced vocal training
needed to develop her voice
properly.

During college Leontyne sang
more and more. Dr. Charles H.
Wesley, president of Wilberforce
College, encouraged her to try for a
professional career. Mrs. Anna M.
Terry, head of the music department,

and Ms. Van Buren also urged
Leontyne to continue her training.
After graduating from college,
Leontyne competed for and won a
scholarship to the renowned Juilliard
School of Music in New York City.

Leontyne's parents were thrilled
when they heard about the
scholarship. Though thankful that
Leontyne and her beautiful voice had
been chosen for such an honor, they
wondered how she was to accept it.
With her brother George now in
college they simply could not afford
to finance a music career for their
daughter.

Help, however, came from some
Laurel friends, the Chisholm family.
They provided enough money to
enable Leontyne to continue

studying music. Through the years, the Price and Chisholm families have kept in close contact and their friendship has remained strong.

Shortly after entering Juilliard, Leontyne became seriously interested in opera. For four years she studied under the direction of Florence Page Kimball, her first formal voice teacher, who remained her teacher and friend even after Leontyne left Juilliard.

Leontyne appeared in many of the school's concerts and operatic productions. During one of these performances at Juilliard, she was heard by composer Virgil Thomson. He asked her to sing the role of St. Cecelia in his opera *Four Saints in Three Acts*.

Scenes from George Gershwin's *Porgy and Bess* that starred
Leontyne Price (as Bess) and William Warfield (as Porgy).
In 1952 the New York cast toured Europe appearing before
enthusiastic audiences in London, Berlin, and other major cities.

This brief Broadway appearance
was so successful that Leontyne was
signed to sing the role of Bess in
George Gershwin's folk opera *Porgy
and Bess.* After appearing in *Porgy
and Bess,* Leontyne was more
determined than ever to succeed in
grand opera.

Leontyne Price sang
the title role in
the opera *Tosca*.

Her next step was to become the first black American to appear in an opera on television. She sang the title role in an NBC production of *Tosca*. Leontyne was chosen for this role not to break racial barriers, but because she was the best singer for the part.

Leontyne made successful debuts in grand opera productions in Europe. She conquered audiences in Paris, Vienna, and London, as well as in the United States. Following these triumphs, Leontyne was invited to star at the Metropolitan Opera in New York, one of the greatest opera houses in the world.

When Leontyne finished singing the role of Leonora in Verdi's *Il Trovatore*, the audience gave her the longest tribute of applause in the Metropolitan Opera's history. The ovation lasted forty-two minutes. We can only imagine what a thrill this must have been for the beautiful young black singer.

Leontyne Price's debut at the Metropolitan Opera
as Leonora in *Il Trovatore,* was hailed by critics
as a "dramatic and a technical triumph." It was
the most applauded moment of the Met season.

After her outstanding debut at the
Metropolitan, Leontyne added
another "first" to her list of
accomplishments. She became the
first black artist to have the honor of
opening a Metropolitan Opera
season.

Seldom in musical history has there been an event as important as the opening night at the new $50 million Metropolitan Opera House at Lincoln Center. To celebrate the occasion, one of America's outstanding composers, Samuel Barber, wrote a new opera, *Antony and Cleopatra*. Tickets quickly sold out, some for as much as $250 each. The part of Cleopatra in this new work was one of the most desired roles ever. There was no question as to which singer would be cast in the role. The choice was obvious — Leontyne Price of Laurel, Mississippi!

Leontyne as Cleopatra (above) and at a benefit concert (below).

Leontyne sang an aria from Verdi's *Il Trovatore* on an NBC television program.

Leontyne appeared as a soloist with the New York Philharmonic Orchestra conducted by Zubin Mehta.

Singing a leading role in one of the world's most famous opera houses on opening night is an honor and the desire of all singers. An even greater honor is to be chosen to open a new opera house. Few singers receive either honor, and fewer still receive both. Receiving both of these honors gave Leontyne Price still more recognition as one of the greatest singers of all time.

Leontyne has been successful off-stage, too. She has received many awards and honors. In 1964 she received the highest American civilian award, the Presidential Freedom Medal, from President Lyndon B. Johnson. She was the first opera singer to be so honored.

She has also received many honorary doctorate degrees from leading universities. Leontyne gives many benefit concerts. One of her benefits helped her mother's former school, Rust College in Mississippi, build a new library. To show its appreciation for Leontyne's efforts, the college named the new library after her.

Leontyne received the Spingarn Medal.

She has received the NAACP
Spingarn Medal for high and noble
achievement by a black American. In
addition to being the subject of
magazine articles, Leontyne Price
has also been featured on magazine
covers. Her recordings have received
eighteen Grammy Awards from the
National Academy of Recording Arts

Leontyne Price sang a duet with Luciano Pavarotti
during the One Hundredth Anniversary Gala of the
Metropolitan Opera in New York City.

and Sciences. She has received three Emmy Awards for her work in television. She also helps to provide music lessons to children in Harlem (New York) at prices they can afford.

Leontyne Price had a strong desire to be a successful opera singer. This goal, along with her unusual vocal ability and stage personality, has led her to great success. Her belief in hard work and her deep religious faith have helped her through difficult periods. The strength of character she has shown during her career marks her as one of America's great women.

ABOUT THE AUTHOR

Sylvia Barkemeyer Williams is library-media specialist at Oak Park School in Laurel, Mississippi, where Leontyne Price attended school. She wrote this book so that children could learn the amazing story of the talented girl who grew up in a small town and became an international opera star.

She holds degrees from William Carey College and the University of Southern Mississippi, both in Hattiesburg, Mississippi. She is married and the mother of two children.